Quest for Wisdom
Lessons for Life

Marsha Ferrick Heiden,
PhD, BCC

The Quest for Wisdom
Lessons for Life

Written by Marsha Ferrick Heiden, PhD, BCC
Photo on cover by Tambako The Jaguar
Tiger in the Grass
https://creativecommons.org/licenses/by-nd/2.0/legalcode

Copyright 2016
All Rights Reserved. No written part of this book can be used or reproduced in any manner whatsoever without written permission.

Marsha Ferrick Heiden, PhD, BCC
Amara Quest, Inc
8322 State Route 305
Garrettsville, OH 44231

In memory of my parents,
Roy Marsh Ferrick & Carolyn Anna Malin,
my greatest teachers

Dedicated to:
Karen

A special thank you to the photographers who so generously posted their fabulous photos an flickr.com for commercial use.

Table of Contents

Introduction...7

Personal: The Journey Within ...15

Life Purpose: The Journey Outward...69

Relationships: The Journey Between...115

Introduction

Quest for Wisdom

The Quest for Wisdom offers pearls of wisdom. Pick up each one exam it, embrace those which work for you. Read them one after the other, or take a specific section personal, life purpose, relationship development. This book has no answers only questions. The wisdom lies within your quiet mind, ponder the point, and you will find your truth.

Read a page or two and think about it then in a day or two read another. They do not need to be read in any order. Write down your thoughts and answers to the questions in the book or in a journal.

The Quest for Wisdom is a source of ideas that assists you in gaining clarity, and authentic connection with yourself, your world, and others. You begin to realize that you can create the life you want through small changes, transcending old patterns that have held you back. Intimacy deepens, enriching your life. You have more choices and options which empower you to continue to change and grow becoming more and more the person you truly are and you can move forward more purposeful and connected then you ever thought possible.

Life is about intimate connections, or lack there of...

Connection with ourselves.

Connection with our lives.

Connections with others.

I can only connect with my life if I am connected with myself.

I can only connect with others to the extent I am connected to myself and to my life.

And others can only connect with me as intimately as they are connected to themselves, and their own lives.

This book is about intimate connection…

To yourself.

To your life.

To others.

What If ...?

Photo by Tambako The Jaguar
Funny Babt Orang utan
https://creativecommons.org/licenses/by-nd/2.0/legalcode

What if every day was lived as a holiday?

What if each day we used our gifts
to make the lives of others better?

What if each day we did this not,
because we should,
but simply because we wanted to...?

What if each day,
we each made a little difference
in someone else's life?

What if...?

Personal

The Journey Within

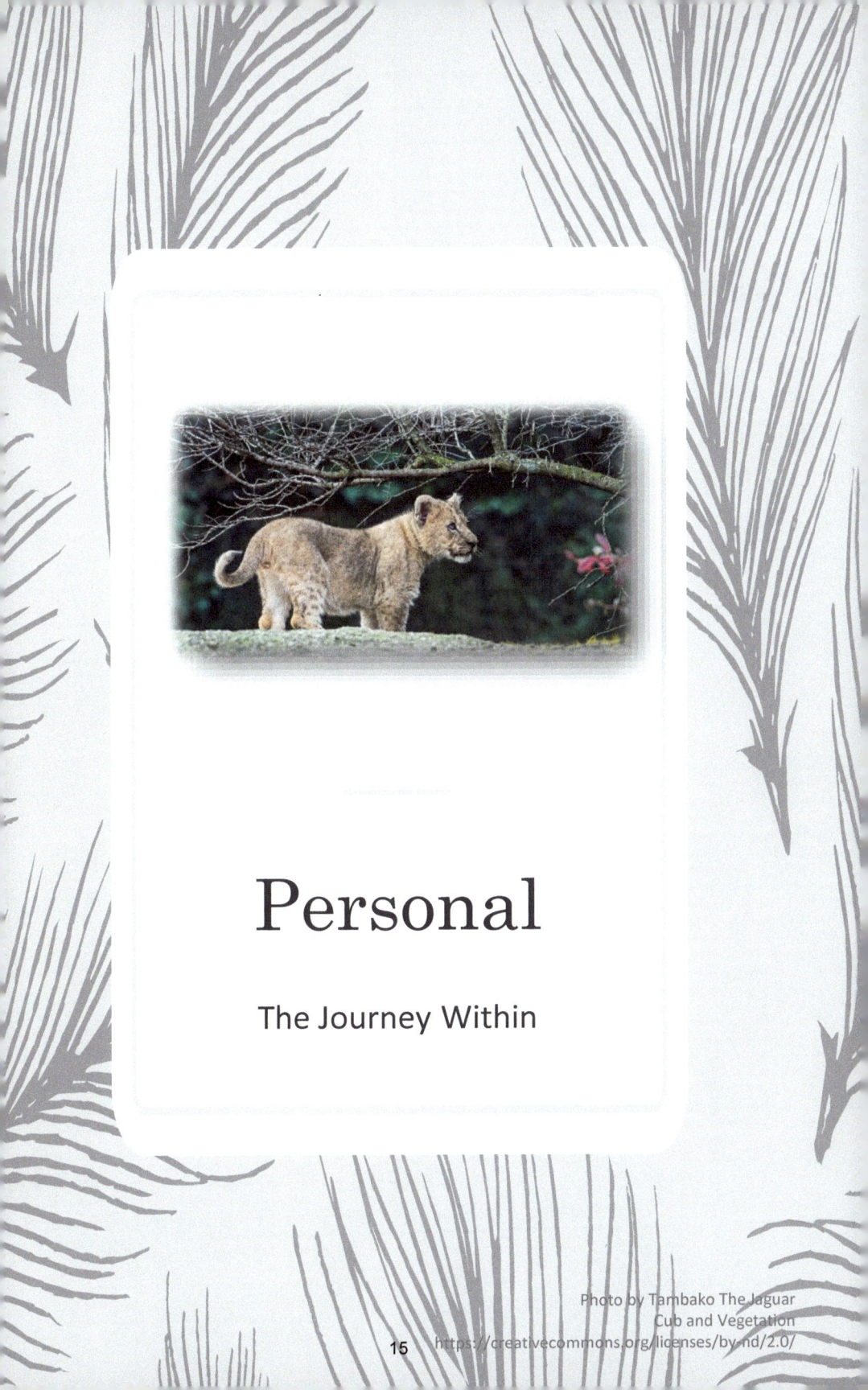

Photo by Tambako The Jaguar
Cub and Vegetation
https://creativecommons.org/licenses/by-nd/2.0/

Dead or Alive?

Photo by Tambako The Jaguar
Eagle in the Flowers
https://creativecommons.org/licenses/by-nd/2.0/

Two flowers side by side,

one is alive, one is dead.

How do you tell the living from the dead?

The dead one has stopped growing.

(paraphrased – W. Dyer)

Are you still growing? Why or why not?

Take Up the Challenge

Photo by Tambako The Jaguar
Climbing Gorilla
https://creativecommons.org/licenses/by-nd/2.0/legalcode

"There is always a gift in any challenge."
Bonnie Ware

Life is a quest, a journey towards fulfillment.
Challenges are opportunities for growth along the way.
No challenges, no growth… you wither away.
Take on the challenge, win or lose, you grow!

What challenge will you take up today?

Risk Pain, Gain Growth!

Photo by Tambako The Jaguar
Cubs Playing Together
https://creativecommons.org/licenses/by-nd/2.0/

And the day came when the risk to remain tight in a bud was more painful than the risk it took to blossom.
Anãis Nin

The transition from the Child Self to the Adult Self requires discipline no matter your age… The good news is that discipline eventually turns into habits that produce a life that is lived with integrity, dignity, elegance, passion, and deep contentment.

The road to your Adult Self is a constant growth process. In the early part of the journey the learning curve is steep and the journey is very difficult and painful. Yet with time you learn that this process is normal that you will survive it, and in fact come to welcome the lessons that you learn. Even when you hurt you know it will be okay. You stop worrying about being hurt and embrace the possibilities knowing that to not risk is far worse then risking and being hurt.

So today embrace what comes your way with the excitement of all the possibilities! What will you risk today?

Reflections

Thoughts and Feelings

I Believe...

Photo by DLB
Per Volar Sunata II
https://creativecommons.org/licenses/by/2.0/legalcode

I create my beliefs about myself. What do I believe that holds me back?

What if I believe...

I can...
 change,
  be whatever I want,
   impact the world,
    change my thoughts, emotions,
view of the world, of others,
     chose to trust or not others.

What if I believe...

I am...
 enough,
  lovable,
   talented,
    intelligent,
     free to choose,
continually changing and growing.

What if I believe...

My feelings are ok.
  create my reality.
    I determine the meaning I give to things.
      I impact all I come in contact with and beyond.
        I trust myself.

What would be my greatest worry if nothing held me back?

Reflections

Look Inside

Face it You're Fallible!

Photo by Ross Gardiner
Zebra Roll
https://creativecommons.org/licenses/by-sa/2.0/legalcode

Do you want to feel better about yourself?

Then ...
Stop judging yourself and others. Find the humor, it is there somewhere. Stay in the moment, yes this moment. Meditate a few minutes each day.

Define 'who you are' by what is in your heart. Take risks, start small, then go big. Address your wants and needs. Cultivate close relationships with people.

Solve and address problems ASAP. Speak positively to yourself, or at least stay neutral. Convert shoulds to coulds. Get balanced meals and exercise.

Change what you can. Mainly your thoughts. Possibly some of your behaviors. Forget the rest.

Learn from your mistakes. Face it you're fallible, and that's ok. Forgive yourself. Move on.

Do this for a year. Who are you now?

Reflections

From Inside

Integrity

Photo by Tambako The Jaguar
Menacing Brown Bear
https://creativecommons.org/licenses/by-nd/2.0/

Integrity...

Awareness.
Honest with self.
Honest with others.

Authentic.
Say what you mean.
Do what you say.
Word and deed align.

Commitment.
Follow through.
Showing up.
Being fully there.

Consistent.
The right thing.
The next right thing.
Even when no one is watching.

Foundation of relationships.
Necessity of self-respect.
Basis of self-esteem.

How is your integrity holding up?

ChChChChanging Today's the Day

Photo by Michael MK Khor
Ready to take off from the cocoon-Atlas Moth
https://creativecommons.org/licenses/by/2.0/legalcode

Energy cannot be created or destroyed, it can only be changed from one form to another.
Albert Einstein

Change comes through cultivation. So to have inner, and outer peace, joy, contentment, a wonder for life, and gratitude then…

Cultivate that change via meditation, sharing meaningfully with others, connecting to all things, accepting what is, and the honest expression of your emotions.

Nothing more or less is required, only continued practice!

What will you practice?

The Journey to Mastery

Photo by Tambako The Jaguar
Posh Female Gorilla Eating
https://creativecommons.org/licenses/by-nd/2.0/

Mastery is not about perfection. It's about a process ... The master is the one that stays on the path day after day, year after year. The master is the one who is willing to try, and fail, and try again, for as long as he or she lives.
George Leonard

What you seek and what you get are often different? Why, because you have mastered habits that help you meet your basic needs, yet do not substantially fulfill you. Consider how you meet your basic need for security, novelty, significance, and connection? Do you meet these needs at the expense of sacrificing your personal growth and contributing to the greater world?

Do you meet these basic needs through habits or addiction such as people pleasing, workaholism, perfectionism, relationships, or a better known addiction such as food, drugs, or alcohol. Do you seek fulfillment in your life, yet you fall short despite your best efforts? Why is that? Why is it you cannot do what you know you need to do? What gets in the way? You do!

You have mastered habits that are getting in your way! You cling to habits that fill your basic needs but hold you back from the continued personal growth you need to master through day to day practice, year after year to be your best self, an awesome life, and to maximize your ability to contribute beyond yourselves to the larger world. How are you holding yourself back? How are the habits you have mastered getting in the way of having the fulfilling life that you want?

What new habits do you need to master? How will you implement these new habits? How will you meet your basic needs while mastering the skills you need to live a fulfilled life?

Write it down. What gets in the way? What needs to be mastered? How do you align your behaviors so that all your needs get met and you master the habits and skills you need to have the awesome life you want?

Master the habits that will meet your basic needs and fulfillment needs both. Consider, reflect, practice, and observe, refine, and begin again. Get rid of habits that do not serve you! Seek and implement habits that do! You will find the life you want!

Reward Yourself

Photo by Tambako The Jaguar
Lion Cubs Doing Nonsense
https://creativecommons.org/licenses/by-nd/2.0/

To be assertive is to be effective and constructive.

Assertiveness requires…

Listening.
Curious questions.
Clarifying.

Validation of the other's perspective.
Slow, soft speaking.
Gentle repetition of what you want.

A nonjudgmental stance.
Patience.
Alternative offers.

Accepting no.
A reward for the smallest achievement.
How will you reward yourself?

A New Way to Look at Emotions

Photo by Peter G W Jones
Osprey 14
https://creativecommons.org/licenses/by-nd/2.0/

Equation of Emotional Management

Emotions = Energy

Emotions create a change in bodily energy.
How will you choose to use it!

You can create
or
You can destroy.

Emotions are an invitation to act that empower you to alter anything you choose for better or worse.

Will you empower yourself?
How will you do it?

Strengthen Your Strengths

Photo by Tambako The Jaguar
Hippo at the Surface
https://creativecommons.org/licenses/by-nd/2.0/

All of us need to begin to think in terms of our own inner strengths, our resilience and resourcefulness, our capacity to adapt and to rely upon ourselves and our families.

Steven Pressfield

It is always easier to strengthen your strengths!

So focus on your strengths.

Transform your strengths into talents, via new experiences.

And your weaknesses? No sweat, delegate them!

List your strengths.

Who are You?

Photo by Tambako The Jaguar
Pretty Brown Owl
https://creativecommons.org/licenses/by-nd/2.0/

Who are you?

How did you answer the question above?

What beliefs do you hold about yourself?

Are those beliefs helpful or hurtful to you?

Do these beliefs move you toward the life you want?

Or do they create obstacles in your mind that limit your possibilities?

You choose what you believe about yourself (*Yes, you really do*).

Is it time to get rid of those unhelpful thoughts?

How will you do it?

Freedom from Fear

Photo by motox810
Redtail Hawl
https://creativecommons.org/licenses/by-nd/2.0/legalcode

Without an open-minded mind, you can never be a great success.
Martha Stewart

Closed minds exist because we are afraid to move out of our comfort zones. We can spot a closed mind by noting excuses, and rationalizations. On the other hand open mindedness comes from natural curiosity and the desire to discover new information. Open mindedness comes from practicing the management of our thoughts through processes such as visualization, affirmations, positive verbalization, acting as if, feeding our minds with the right stuff, associating with positive people, and by teaching others what you learn.

Today how can you open your mind 5% more?

Attitude Adoption

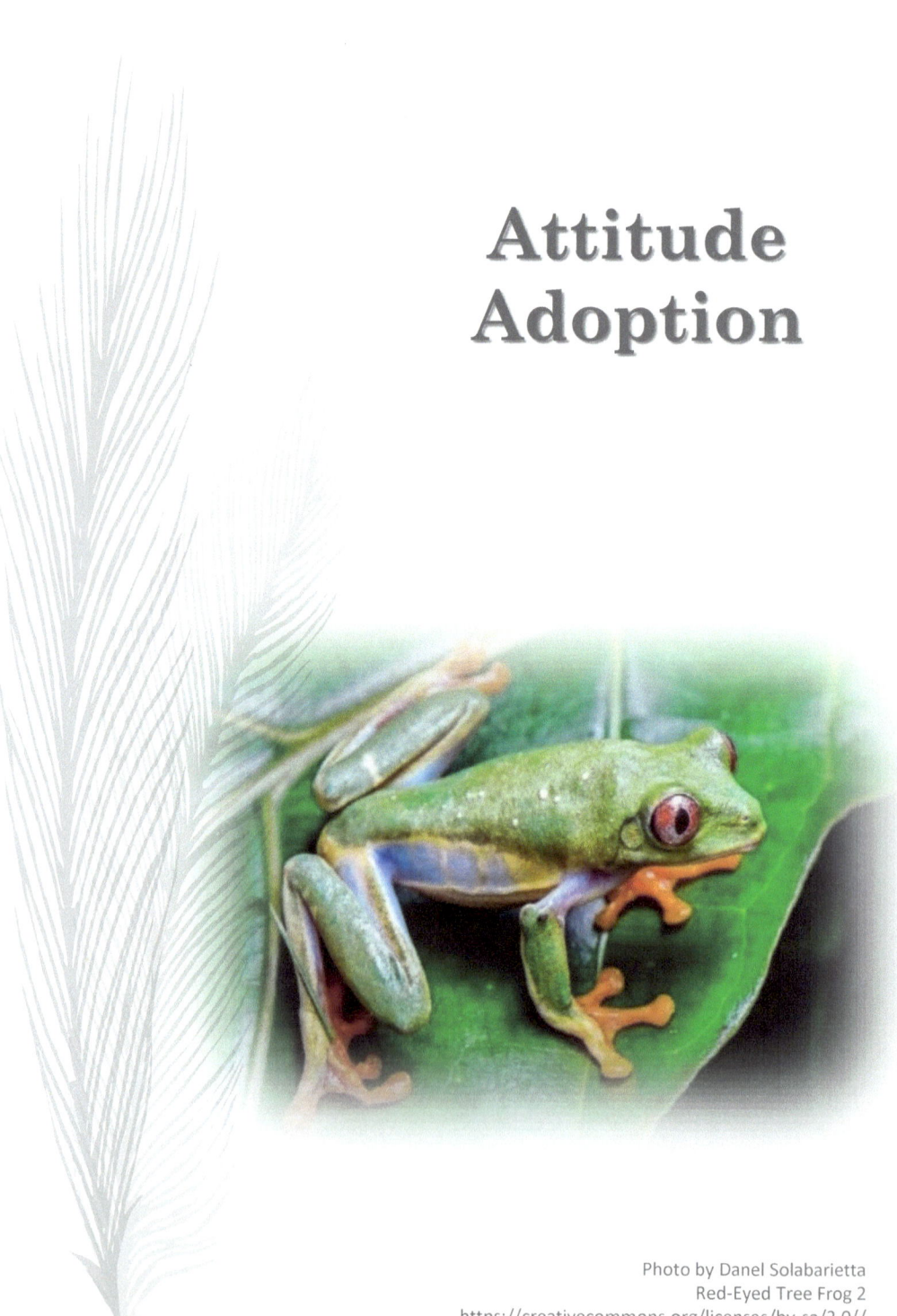

Photo by Danel Solabarietta
Red-Eyed Tree Frog 2
https://creativecommons.org/licenses/by-sa/2.0//

Nothing can stop the man with the right mental attitude from achieving his goal; nothing on earth can help the man with the wrong mental attitude.
Thomas Jefferson

The attitude you adopt will determine your success in creating the life you want. Positive attitudes equal positive outcomes!

How can you change your attitude?

Harnessing Stress

Photo by Justin Jensen
"Bonger"
https://creativecommons.org/licenses/by/2.0/legalcode

Stress is an inside job.
It lives inside you.
Nowhere else.
It is an internal energy
that helps you get things done.
An internal physiological response.
Harness the benefits of stress.
Accept that change is constant.
Problems are challenges
Hold a positive orientation.
Be flexible.
Tolerate ambiguity.
Focus on what you can control.
Don't get derailed.
Be 100% responsible for your responses.
Don't take on anyone else's stress.
Influence the events you can positively.
Prioritize self-care.
Debrief.
Continually update your skills.
Experiment with fresh approaches.
You create stress. You contain stress.
You control stress.

How will you manage your stress differently now that you understand it is an inside job?

Creating Your Desires

Photo by Tambako The Jaguar
Oskar Running in the Snow I
https://creativecommons.org/licenses/by-nd/2.0/legalcode

> *All actions result from thought*
> *so it is thoughts that matter.*
> Sai Baba

We are our thoughts. Our thoughts change our biochemistry so our thinking creates who we are becoming.

The thoughts we have about ourselves have the most impact. These thoughts influence how we treat ourselves, and in turn that teaches others how to treat us. Thoughts are an informational energy field. This intelligent power results from trillions of messenger molecules that inform each of our cells precisely how to function, thus our positive thoughts create positive energy, and vice versa.

So the wonderful news is that we always have a choice about what we think, when we think, whether we think, or whether we don't. So we can consciously choose our thoughts, which allows us the ability to control our lives from the inside out. Given this reality we can create anything we desire.

Are your thoughts aligned with what you would like to create today?

History, Make You or Break You?

Photo by Stuart Webster
New Forest Foal
https://creativecommons.org/licenses/by/2.0/legalcode

> *Who has fully realized*
> *that history is not contained*
> *in thick books but lives in our very blood?*
> Carl Jung

How you view your history will determine your future. Consider your history, tragic or not as a place of valuable lessons learned. Whether your past taught you what to do, or not to do it has impacted you. Remember under pressure coal becomes diamonds, and therefore your experiences are now a precious resource to create the present, and the future you desire. So go, mine the diamonds from your history. Now create the present and future you want. Start now, create the day you want today. What will it look like?

Reconsider Your Values!

Photo by Eric Kilby
Giraffe Portrait
https://creativecommons.org/licenses/by-sa/2.0/legalcode

You're living life from your values, right? Right.

Uncomfortable with your life? Not where you want to be? Not achieving your goals or desires? Is your behavior destructive to yourself or others?

Consider your values… Who's values are you living?

Hook, line, and sinker you bought into Mom and Dad's values. Possibly you are still living the values of your adolescence, living in rebellion to those you perceive are in power. Living the values of today's friends. Your church's values. The corporation where you work. Perhaps your spouse's or your community's values.

Yet are any of these really your values? Yes.

Are you certain? Maybe….No.

Make a list of your values.

Ask yourself, is this a standard I want to live by today. Yes! Great keep it. No! Get rid of it. Not sure. Write it down, contemplate it. Get clear on it, then stash it or toss it.

Choose values that are yours then start living in alignment with your values today, and behave accordingly. Don't be surprised if life gets easier. As you move towards your goals, and gain your desires, your behavior becomes constructive for yourself and others.

Funny how living in alignment with our own values thrusts us forward into the life we want! Where are you out of alignment?

Reflections

From Inside

Do You Verbally Abuse Yourself?

Others?

Photo by Tambako The Jaguar
Pygmy Hippo with Open Mouth
https://creativecommons.org/licenses/by-nd/2.0/

"The old saying about sticks and stones was wrong. Names will forever hurt you," says Natalie Sachs-Ericsson a pychologist and researcher. We often consider this verbal abuse if it is done to us by others, yet take a step back and *"consider all the hurtful things you say to yourself (and/or your children, colleagues, friends) during the course of a day. Those disparaging comments you inflict on yourself will forever hurt you (and others)"* writes life coach Joelene Ashker.

So, STOP with the negative comments to yourself and everyone else. It's that simple. STOP. Forgive yourself. Replace it with a truth based on the facts of who you are today, not who you were, or who you told yourself you were, or who someone else told you that you were but actually who you are...today. Do it NOW.

Do it EVERY TIME...until you do it without thinking about it. What you focus on you become.

Focus on being worthless, you will become worthless. Focus on your value and your value will grow.

Remember you are in charge of your own garden!

Pull out the weeds, and plant the seeds you want to grow!

What seeds shall you grow?

Reflections

From Inside

To Create a Great Relationship, Be a Great You!

Photo courtesy of Brendon Kipini
Ambrogio, Lusitano Stallion
Spring Wood Farm

This may be stating the obvious, but if you want a great relationship you have to be a great you! Not a good you, but a great you. If your relationships are not what you want them to be then consider the possibility that you are not being the best you, you can be. Not everyone is capable of having great relationships. However, if a great relationship is something you want then you have to be capable of having a great relationships on your side of the table. There is an old saying, *2's and 10's do not marry* (and if they do they divorce quickly). People with vast differences in awareness, insight, and relationship skills do not have meaningful relationships together ever. They may be acquaintances or even friends, but they do not have deep, meaningful interpersonal relationships.

If your belief in yourself, your personal growth, attitude, and relationship skills are not the best then don't expect to have awesome relationships. If you want great relationships read books, watch DVDs, attend seminars, and focus each day on working to be a better you within each relationship.

Bring the best you to your relationships, only then do you have a chance at having great relationships.

How will you improve your you?

Life Purpose

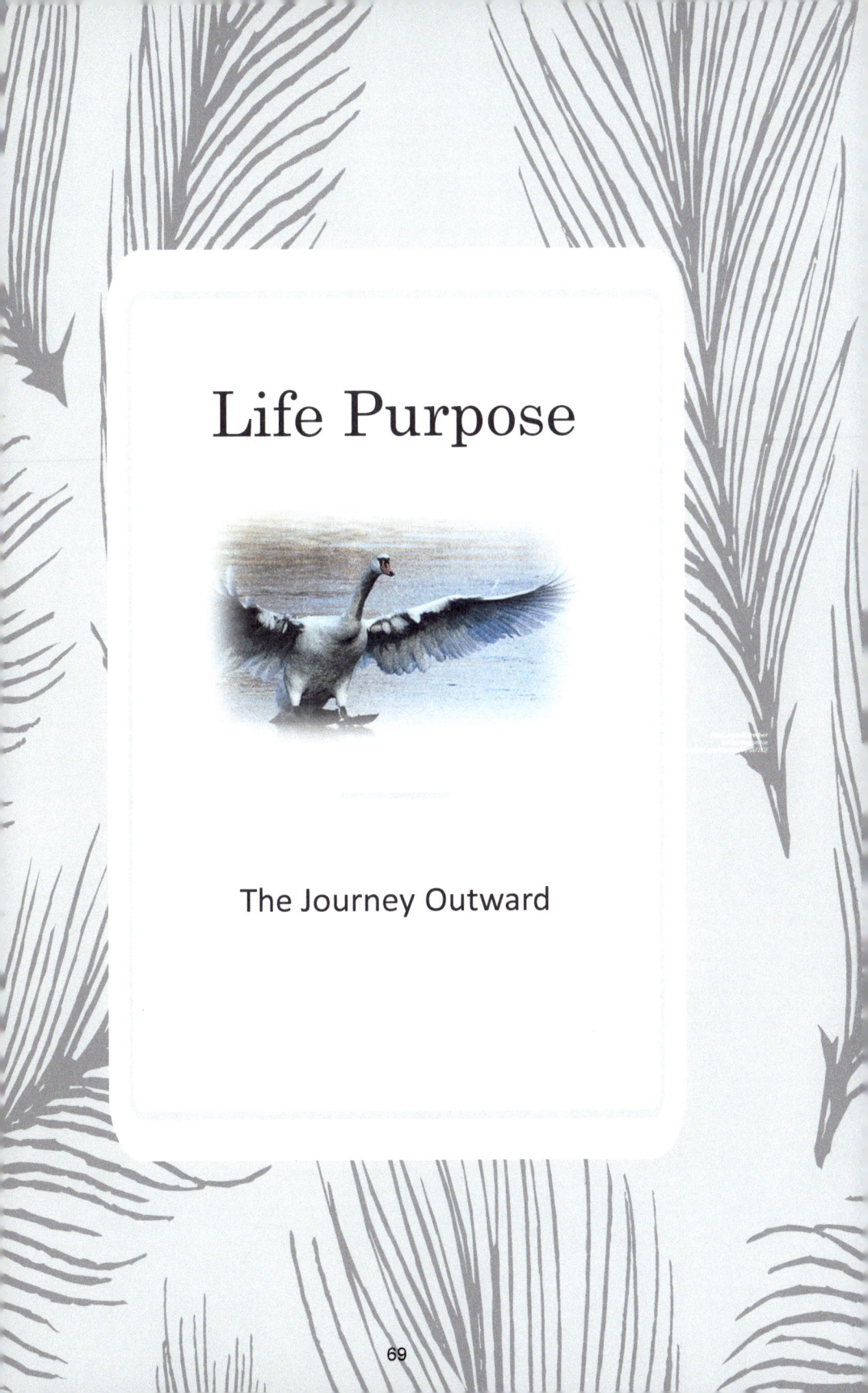

The Journey Outward

The Gift of Responsibility

Photo by Tony Hisgett
Baby Orangutan 2
https://creativecommons.org/licenses/by/2.0/legalcode

Responsibility vs Expectations

'Expectations' are responsibilities that we complete while 'Responsibility' is a gift that requires personal accountability, and the freedom to consciously choose thoughts, actions, and feelings.

'Responsibility' recognizes that success and happiness are created within. Living fully and completely while pursuing a fulfilling life path is empowering, and one of the greatest gifts received from choosing the 'Responsibility' of directing our own lives.

Have you given yourself the gift of 'Responsibility'?

Is Your Life a Wandering Generality?

Photo by Deepak
Trotting Along the Winding Path
https://creativecommons.org/licenses/by/2.0/legalcode

Without purpose, your life becomes a *"wandering generality,"* according to Patrick Williams and Lloyd J. Thomas. When Carnegie wrote, *"I am going to spend the first forty years of my life creating a fortune, and the second forty years giving it all away,"* he was articulating a clear and focused life path. Yet unlike Carnegie many of us live a life of meaningless wandering.

Figuring out which path or purpose to follow can be an overwhelming task. Have you ever thought, *"I have no idea what my life purpose is supposed to be? How do I figure out what my purpose is supposed to be? I have lost my life purpose, or completed my life purpose, now what? Why am I alive in this time, this place?"*

If so consider meditating on the following, write down whatever comes to mind first!

What motivates me? What energizes me? What brings me pleasure? What do I really want? Who do I enjoy? What would I do with my life, if my family would and could support anything I chose to do? If I had no family members to consider what would my future plans be? If I had three months, no obligations, and no financial limitations what would I do with my time? If I had only six months to live how would I spend it? If I were granted five wishes, what would I ask for?

Contemplate your answers. Are you on your path?

Reflections

From Your Life

Vision or Circumstance?

Photo by smerikal
Bestineo
https://creativecommons.org/licenses/by-sa/2.0/

You are not here merely to make a living. You are here in order to enable the world to live more amply, with greater vision, with a finer spirit of hope and achievement. You are here to enrich the world, and you impoverish yourself if you forget the errand.
Woodrow Wilson

What will create your future? Vision or circumstance?

When you create a vision of your future, you will do the things you need to do to get there.

Vision or circumstances will create your future.

Which will you choose? Why?

Will We Act from Love or Live in Fear?

Photo by Ryan Li
In the Big Storm
https://creativecommons.org/licenses/by/2.0/legalcode

My experience of life is that it is truly a remarkable journey. It involves peaceful highways, mountainous roads, barren wastelands, magical sunsets, and torrential floods yet around every corner there is something new to see and lessons learned along the way. As I think back on my own life I am in wonder at how it has unfolded. Struggles and dark times have taught me valuable lessons for current days. I choose each day to continue down the road fearless about the future because I have overcome and learned from the past.

I have many lessons yet to learn, however life's experiences have taught me that it truly *"is the journey and not the destination"* that matters. Don't get me wrong I am a goal setter, and passionate about reaching the goals I seek. I have a vision for the future yet am flexible enough to understand there is an energy greater than myself that allows me to live out a life of even greater success if I allow it to manifest itself through me. There are times I have watched my life demand of me that I live out a life of passion or risk an emotional and psychological death from living a life of mediocrity. This demand for growth though painful can be as difficult as a death or divorce, or as simple as a friend telling me the kind truth.

A kind truth is one that I do not always want to hear but definitely need to hear. I have learned from these lessons that I can tolerate the pain that comes with growth. These lessons continue to provide me with the richest rewards. As I grow my ability to love, serve, and deeply connect with others multiplies.

Today for me living a successful life of passion and service is no longer an option on my quest. It is in the words of Bette Midler's song, The Rose… "it is a hunger, An endless aching need".

The journey of my life has lead me here to this time and to this place for a reason. The road before me may have peaceful highways, mountainous roads, barren wastelands, magical sunsets, and torrential floods, yet I am ready to live it fully, fearlessly with passion and determination because of what I have learned on the road thus far that continuing this journey means I will continue to learn, grow and serve along life's highway seeking each golden lining, each rainbow, and every brass ring that comes my way with joy! Each challenge will be a gift and a creative opportunity that I will embrace with all the grace I possess. I am committing to making my choices and actions based on love not fear today.

How will you chose to live this day?

Reflections

From Your Life

Choose One!

Photo by Tambako The Jaguar
So Many Fruits!
https://creativecommons.org/licenses/by-nd/2.0/

Today I choose life. Every morning when I wake up I can choose joy, happiness, negativity, pain... To feel the freedom that comes from being able to continue to make mistakes and choices - today I choose to feel life, not to deny my humanity but embrace it.

Kevyn Aucoin

Make a list of what you want to explore, visit, study, learn, do, photograph, read, write, meet, or see!

Choose one!

Set a date!

Make a strategy!

Go for it!

Where will you start?

Finding Success!

Photo by Hans Splinter
White Horse
https://creativecommons.org/licenses/by-nd/2.0/legalcode

Success is not the key to happiness. Happiness is the key to success. If you love what you are doing, you will be successful.

Albert Schweitzer

Success, the state of contentment that you experience on your journey to who you want to be.

Your contentment expands as you embrace your life ever more fully!

How can you embrace your life more fully today?

Out of the Box

Photo by Mike Boswell
Tree Swallow Pair at Nesting Box
https://creativecommons.org/licenses/by/2.0/legalcode

Creative thinking – in terms of idea creativity – is not a mystical talent. It is a skill that can be practised and nurtured.
Edward de Bono

To have the life you want you will need to think creatively. Creative thinking is a skill that can be learned. Thinking creatively requires looking beyond your normal thinking. Out of the box thinking requires making novel combinations, metaphors, analogies, taking on a different world view, make unique connections, disconnect typical connections, make reversals, do the opposite, view it from a different angle, look for the exceptions, the accidental, look for what you were not looking for, write everything down without judgment, elaborate on every idea, allow your subconscious to work. Then create the life you want.

When will you start? Where do you need to think out of the box?

It's a Goal!

Photo by Kat and Rully
Baby Zebra
https://creativecommons.org/licenses/by-sa/2.0/legalcode

Arise! Awake!
and stop not until the goal is reached.
Swami Vivekananda

You have your goal!

Now you need a strategy!

Create a written or visual picture of the outcome you want.

Make a list of actions you will need to take to get there.

What help will you need? How have others achieved this goal? Make a to do list for the first action you need to take. Then complete the first step on your list. You are on your way to your GOAL!

What is your first step?

Are Your Actions Successful?

Photo by Tambako The Jaguar
The Baby Elephant Playing with Water
https://creativecommons.org/licenses/by-nd/2.0/legalcode

Action is a great restorer and builder of confidence. Inaction is not only the result, but the cause, of fear. Perhaps the action you take will be successful; perhaps different action or adjustments will have to follow. But any action is better than no action at all.
Norman Vincent Peale

Successful actions are empowered choices that require deliberate consciousness, open-mindedness, and personal integrity.

Are your actions successful?

You're a Leader!

Photo by Bureau of Land Management Oregon and Washington
Beaty Butte Wild Horse Gather, 2015
https://creativecommons.org/licenses/by/2.0/legalcode

A leader is one who knows the way, goes the way, and shows the way.
John C. Maxwell

We are always leading someone. Primarily ourselves, but also others.

How are you leading your chosen life?

How are you a leader for others?

Are Commitment and Persistence Synonyms?

Photo by Steven Lilley
Running
https://creativecommons.org/licenses/by-sa/2.0/legalcode

Nothing in this world can take the place of persistence. Talent will not: nothing is more common than unsuccessful men with talent. Genius will not; unrewarded genius is almost a proverb. Education will not: the world is full of educated derelicts. Persistence and determination alone are omnipotent.
Calvin Coolidge

What we commit to we accomplish if we persist. Are your commitments continually challenged?

If so recommit to your goals. Refocus on them. Remind yourself of your desired outcome. Keep visual reminders close by. Reward yourself for progress. Overcome obstacles with strategies. Maintain actions that support your goal. Persist, Persist, Persist!

How will you persist?

All We Have!

Photo by William Warby
Elephant Seals
https://creativecommons.org/licenses/by/2.0/legalcode

Each moment is perfect and heaven-sent, in that each moment holds the seeds for growth.
Suzan-Lori Parks

Time is simply a concept, a mental construct.

So direct experience really only exists in this moment, where there is no past, and no future, so all we have is right now.

Make the most of it!

What can you do to make the most of each moment?

Make it a Must or Toss it!

Photo by Tambako The Jaguar
Omysha and the Branch
https://creativecommons.org/licenses/by-nd/2.0/

Want to get organized?

Make the most of your time?

Make a list of all you have to do. Yes, everything! Take three pieces of paper. Label them…

Must Do, Should Do, Not Yet. Leave the *Must Do* out.

That is the stuff you are committing to doing. Throw out the *Should Do* list. You are not committed to it and you are not going to do it. Put the *Not Yet* list aside.

When the time is right you will add those items to your *Must Do* list. Take an hour simplify your life. Make more time to create the life you want instead of filling it with meaningless tasks.

Dynamic Balance

Photo by Andy McLemore
Over There Guys! (Fractalized)
https://creativecommons.org/licenses/by-sa/2.0/legalcode

Success, although personally defined is obtained only when one leads a dynamically balanced life that prioritizes life responsibilities in this way...

1. Self-Care and Self-Responsibility
2. Partner Relationship
3. Parent/Child Relationship(s)
4. Friendships
5. Career/Work/Job

If your road to success is strewn with obstacles consider for a moment, where do you spend your time?

Are You Productive or Just Busy?

Photo by Sharon Mollerus
Busy Bee
https://creativecommons.org/licenses/by/2.0/

Excessive busyness is a form of show business. It has no place in the real world of straight-line effectiveness.
Dusan Djujukich

Finally, I have cut through the cr**, if I am too busy I am not being productive period!

Productive work reduces busyness it does not increases it. Sure being busy sounds good. It looks good, but it really is about going around and around without really getting anywhere.

Stop! For just a minute stop.

Think! What really must be done today? Why? Does it add to the bottom line? Does it improve a relationship? Is it really productive?

Is your time being spent in real conversations with amazing people that will make things happen? Or is your time wasted in lazy mental busyness tasks or conversations about things that will never happen?

So, next time you say you "are too busy", join me in asking yourself why? Why am I busy? Why aren't I being productive? What am I avoiding by being busy? Why am I getting in the way of my own success?

Reflections

From Your Life

What You Do?

Photo by Richard Walker
Owl in Flight
https://creativecommons.org/licenses/by/2.0/legalcode

Success demands singleness of purpose. You need to be doing fewer things for more effect instead of doing more things with side effects. It is those who concentrate on but one thing at a time who advance in this world...When people look back on their lives, it is the things they have not done that generate the greatest regret...People's actions may be troublesome initially; it is their inactions that plague them most with long-term feelings of regret. Make sure every day you do what matters most. When you know what matters most, everything makes sense. When you don't know what matters most, anything makes sense.

Gary Keller

If this were your last year left on this earth, and you could only do one thing in the year that remained using only your current resources, "What one thing would you do? When would you do it? With whom would you do it?"

Now write it down in this format, *"I am visiting Disneyland with my children, August 1-10th, XXXX."* Fill in the blanks...*I am* _____ *with* _____ *on/by (date)* _____.

Create a *To Do List* to make this event happen. Determine the first step, and take it, then the next, and the next...before long we will see you at Disney, or where ever your vision takes you!

What will you do this year?

Reflections

From Your Life

Spotting the Spiritual

Photo by Dawn Beattie
Allen's Hummingbird (selasphorus sasin)
https://creativecommons.org/licenses/by/2.0/legalcode

...Spiritual opening is not a withdrawal to some imagined realm or safe cave. It is not a pulling away, but a touching of all the experience of life with wisdom and with a heart of kindness, without any separation.
Jack Kornfield

The spiritual is subtle. To see it look for...

An extraordinary ease and grace that others want. Actions that are the next right thing, without concern for self, results or outcomes. Roots in rich soil, yet with the resilience to withstand toxicity without being tainted by it. Blissfulness that attracts the spiritual. Simple living that assumes abundance, and is generous. Quick learning and responding, connecting in loving ways. No talk just actions that align with spiritual living.

Can you see what is spiritual now? What is it?

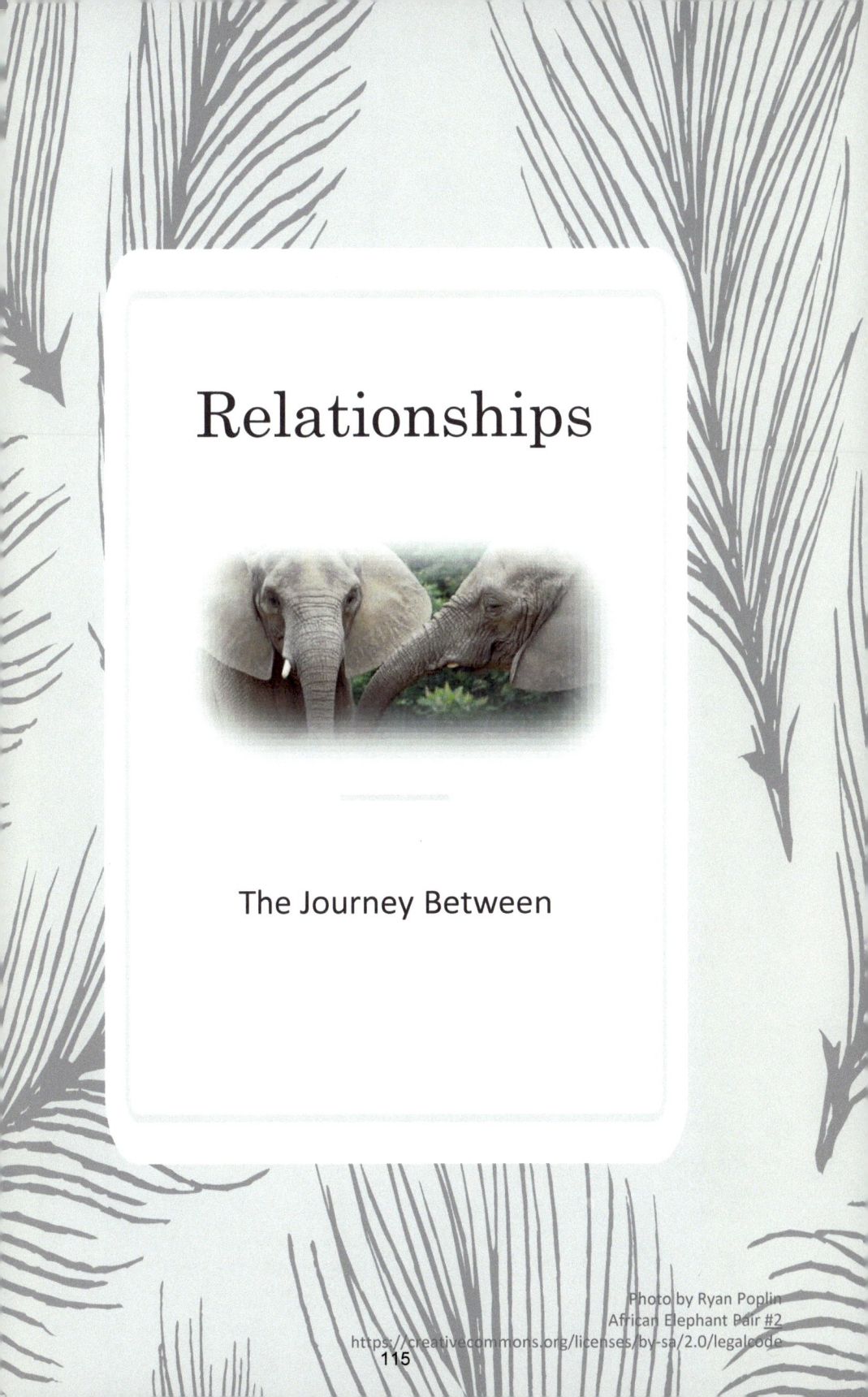

Intimacy in Relationships through Deeper Human Connectedness

Photo by Filipia Machado
African Animals @ Bioparc Valencia
https://creativecommons.org/licenses/by/2.0/legalcode

What does it mean to live in connection? It means I am connected to myself, I have intrapersonal intimacy, I know myself. I am aware of my thoughts, feelings, and behaviors. I take responsibility for and seek to understand them. I am responsible for myself, and blaming my thoughts, feelings, and behaviors on others is a cop out that dismisses me from personal responsibility. Likewise, I am not responsible for the thoughts, feelings, and behaviors of others; they are responsible for their own.

To live in connection means that I am also able to experience interpersonal intimacy, a connection between me and others at a fundamental level of being. I allow myself to be known, they allow themselves to be known and we are both aware that this connection is occurring. This level of connection is exquisitely deep, fleeting, and quite rare. My experience with this type of connection is of being suspended in a time and place where the world around us falls away, and all that is left is the deep, exhilarating, and sometimes terrifying experience of knowing and being known.

To live in connection means that I am willing to develop skills to listen to and understand myself and others deeply, and that I have others in my life that are willing to be known and to know me. Many believe they desire this depth of connection, yet few are willing to do the work it takes to achieve it. It is frightening to look at oneself, unmasked and vulnerable and it is even more terrifying to let others see our essence. It is also amazingly rewarding and awesome to be seen, known, and still loved.

If I am to live in connection with others it means I cannot shrink from the authenticity and vulnerability of them. I must value the courage it takes others to let me know them. In turn, I must not shy away from truly knowing them, honoring their journey, and holding their space with the sacredness it deserves.

I cannot flinch if I am repulsed by what they have done or what has been done to them, because in those moments of true connection I must be able to support their truth, not indulge my own weaknesses and be able to love them more by knowing them for who they truly are. By knowing and connecting, we form meaning for our own lives and celebrate the lives of others.

Making Meaning
Why Collaborated Experience is Essential

Photo by Steve Wilson
Mandrill Face
https://creativecommons.org/licenses/by/2.0/legalcode

The act of making meaning is fascinating. It is a perspective from which I choose to tell my story and it defines my role in an interaction. It determines the path I take next, and impacts my world and those in it. Making meaning can strengthen relationships or destroy them. Let me give you an example. I call a friend. She doesn't return the call. Why? My mind flips though possibilities, each a rich, scripted story in my imagination that I can use to make sense of the situation.

I think, "She is busy. She is injured or in the hospital. She is depressed. I am not important enough for her to call back. She is out of the country. She hates me.

Which story is true? The reality is, I don't know. But that doesn't stop me from fcreating possibilities in my mind. The story I choose is important because the story I use to create meaning will determine both my attitude and my future behavior toward my friend.

If I believe the story she hates me then I might think "poor me" and become sad about the loss of the relationship. If I believe the story that she is injured or in the hospital then I might panicked, and anxious and call all the local hospitals to see if she has been admitted. If I believe she is busy or out of the country then I might do nothing, and wait for her to contact me.

What I could do is say, "Wow! That's interesting she didn't call me back. Hmmm... I wonder why. I'll find out. I'll call her back, stop at her house, leave a message at her office, or call a mutual friend to see if she has heard from her.

Any of these scenarios or others might be true. But without more data, I cannot identify the true meaning, nor make an an accurate choice from among the many possibilities.

So let's say that I choose to collect more data. I stop at my friend's house and ask if she received my call. She responds "Yes, but I decided not to return it because I'm upset with you." I decide to explore her response rather than immediately reacting with defensiveness. "Oh! Why are you upset with me?" She says, "Because you stood me up for dinner last Thursday night."

Now I have enough data to construct an authentic, shared meaning of the situation, plus an opportunity to apologize and try to repair the relationship. If, however, I had not chosen to get her perspective, I would not have been able to create a shared meaning with my friend. And without this shared meaning, the relationship would possibly remain damaged. I would miss an opportunity to reconnect, and repair our relationship.

Uncovering a shared meaning takes work and risk. It means facing truths I may not want to hear about myself, my faults, and my shortcomings. However, setting my ego aside allows me to nurture and repair the relationships in my life. I can write a lone script, or I can write a story that encompasses the perspective of others.

If the script I write of my own life is without the perspective of others it will read very differently than the one I co-create with others. The choices I make are dependent upon my willingness to view life through multiple lenses. If I choose to be an adult and to be responsible for my life and my impact on others, rather than give into my ego's perspective then I will write a story that is authentic and corroborated. This richer, fuller story will embrace the differences in perspectives, truths and will deepen my relationships with others.

Where will you begin to rewrite your stories?

Photo by Linda Yvonne
Love's Old Sweet Song
https://creativecommons.org/licenses/by/2.0/legalcode

Character Matters to Quality in a Relationship

Photo by Jonathan Leung
Handsome Guy
https://creativecommons.org/licenses/by-sa/2.0/legalcode

The quality of your life is the quality of your relationships.
Anthony Robbins

The quality of our lives my be the quality of our relationships, however the quality of a relationship is based on the character of the individuals involved in that relationship. Successful relationships are formed by individuals with characteristics that enable the relationship to thrive.

What characteristics help your relationships thrive?

What characteristics do you want to develop in yourself?

Relationship Makers or Breakers

Photo by Peter G W Jones
Red Deer 20
https://creativecommons.org/licenses/by-nd/2.0/legalcode

If we have no peace, it is because we have forgotten that we belong to each other.
Mother Theresa

Relationships are about belonging. What makes or breaks a relationship? Belonging is a major component of maintaining a relationship. Belonging is an emotional connection with others that creates an inner peace. So, how do I know I belong?

I belong when someone…
– pays attention to what I am saying and doing.
– really hears what I am saying.
– empathizes with the story I am telling.
– can reflect the essence of what I am sharing.
– respects my words, thoughts, and beliefs.
– accepts me as I am without trying to change me.
– honors the boundaries I assert.
– can share who they are with me.
– can tolerate my directness without distress.

How do you know when you belong?

Principles of Great Relationships

Photo by WisconsinKow
Penguins in Love
https://creativecommons.org/licenses/by/2.0/legalcode

Do not do unto others as you expect they should do unto you. Their tastes may not be the same.
George Bernard Shaw

Certainly, the Golden Rule has value yet Shaw's quote makes us reflect on the principles of great relationships. The basic principles of great relationships, according to Williams and Thomas, are to remember that people are different, so treat them accordingly. Next, build the esteem of others which motivates them through love, and not fear. Love is far more potent. Third, interact with others using purposeful behavior considering the facts before you, and absent habitual reactions of the past. Last, remember that when we like ourselves, we like others, and others like us.

Which principle will you focus on to take your relationship from good to great today?

Extraordinary Relationships

Photo by Tambako The Jaguar
Snuggling Tiger Couple
https://creativecommons.org/licenses/by-nd/2.0/

Creating extraordinary relationships requires regular emotional deposits, and minimal withdrawals.
Stephen Covey

Who doesn't want extraordinary relationships? I love my extraordinary relationships. Don't you? What makes them extraordinary? Emotional deposits are one thing that makes a relationship extraordinary.

When am I making emotional deposits? When I create acts of kindness, keep promises, have and honor clear agreements, speak well of others in their absence, apologize, and forgive. However, it is not enough to just make emotional deposits I must minimize emotional withdrawals. Emotional withdrawals can be acts of unkindness, broken promises, unclear expectations or non-existent agreements, disloyal in word or deed, never apologizing, or never forgiving.

Are you making more emotional deposits than withdrawals in your relationships? Are you wondering why your relationships are not extraordinary? What actions will you take to make more emotional deposits today in order to begin to make your relationships extraordinary?

Photo by Hunter Desportes
DSCN 9526
https://creativecommons.org/licenses/by/2.0/legalcode

Humanity is Borne

Empathy is about finding echoes of another person in yourself.
Mohsin Hamid

Empathy is the of sensitivity to your own and another's experience.

Empathy...

Heals. Increases integrity. Makes you complete.

Through empathy humanity is borne.

How do you measure your humanity?

Both Given & Received

Photo by US Fish and Wildlife Service Headquarters
So Many Fruits!
https://creativecommons.org/licenses/by/2.0/legalcode

Giving opens the way for receiving.
Florence Scovel Shinn

Create a fulfilling life then...
Share your life with someone to help fulfill their life...

This sharing entails both...

　Giving and receiving at the same time.
　It will build an effective relationships.
　Providing for win-win outcomes.
　Abundance shared is an act of love.

Generosity, both a gift given and received.

Where will you start?

How to be Honest

Photo by Joanne Goldby
Shetlands -2874.jpg
https://creativecommons.org/licenses/by-sa/2.0/

There are no facts, only interpretations.
Friedrich Nietzsche

Recognize your truth is not necessarily everyone else's truth. Be aware of the way you filter facts.

Temper your truth with tact. Be congruent. Follow through. Create connection by valuing your and the other's interest as equal.

Be trustworthy, and trouble free.

What truth are you ignoring?

Can Conflict be Creative?

Photo by Tambako The Jaguar
Mohan
https://creativecommons.org/licenses/by-nd/2.0/legalcode

Peace is not the absence of conflict but the presence of creative alternatives for responding to conflict - alternatives to passive or aggressive responses, alternatives to violence.
Dorothy Thompson

Win-Win is the outcome sought after in most conflict resolution strategies, but often we resort to compromise.

Compromise is where everyone gives up something, not really the win-win we are seeking.

What we really want is creative synthesis. Creative synthesis is where everyone's abilities, values, expertise are validated and respected. Each persons wishes, wants, needs, and positions are clear. Each person can support their own and the other's position. Through the use of collective energy, solutions are developed so that both parties get what they want.

Now that is what I call Win-Win! Where can you create a win-win today?

Synergistic Relationships are Superior

Photo by Tambako The Jaguar
Playing Elephants
https://creativecommons.org/licenses/by-nd/2.0/legalcode

"Synergy the interaction or cooperation of two or more organizations, substances, or other agents to produce a combined effect greater than the sum of their separate effects."
Google

A synergistic relationship occurs when two people create a greater contribution together than they would independently. Synergistic relationships are based on co-creating outcomes. In synergistic relationships each person inquires about they other. They are interested and curious about each other and their world. They focus on fully comprehending the other, before sharing their own ideas. They speak with clarity and appreciation of the other's position and gifts. They understand that timing is crucial in co-creating greater outcomes together.

Reflect Responsibly

Photo by Peter G W Jones
Grey Squirrel 2
https://creativecommons.org/licenses/by-nd/2.0/legalcode

Feedback, when given well, should not alienate the receiver of the feedback, but should motivate him/her to perform better.
Unknown

Rules for reflecting behavior.

1. Give it only when solicited.
    -Or at least ask if they want feedback first!
2. Describe do not evaluate.
    -Criticism is never well received.
3. Be specific not general.
    -Specificity has meaning.
4. Take into account your needs **and** those of the receiver.
    -Or it will fall on deaf ears.
5. Direct it toward behavior which the receiver can change.
    -Otherwise what is the point!
6. Time it well.
    -In the midst of an emotional crisis feedback is never well received.
7. Have the receiver mirror it back.

Reflecting your reflection keeps the mirror clean! What are you reflecting?

Perfect Listening

Photo by Don Graham
Wild Burros, San Timoteo Canyon 7-12
https://creativecommons.org/licenses/by-nd/2.0/legalcode

"People love to talk but hate to listen. Listening is not merely not talking, though even that is beyond most of our powers; it means taking a vigorous, human interest in what is being told us. You can listen like a blank wall or like a splendid auditorium where every sound comes back fuller and richer."
A.D. Miller

The perfect listener concentrates, stays present and opens all her senses and engages in the collection of outside information.

The perfect listener has a blank mind without filters, judgments or biases.

The perfect listener hears what is and isn't said.

The perfect listener understands that the speaker is always right in her world.

The perfect listener is curious.

The perfect listener learns from everyone, including herself.

How do you know you are listening?

Are You Understood?

Photo by Alexandre Alacchi
Dog
https://creativecommons.org/licenses/by/2.0/legalcode

> A genius knows how to make himself easily understood without being obvious about it.
> — J. Anouilh

To be understood.

Pause.
Breathe.
    Be direct.
    Keep it short.
    Keep it simple.

Make actions, coincide.
Chances are you will be understood!

How are you a genius in communicating?

Between the Lines

Photo by Tambako The Jaguar
Zebra Looking to Side
https://creativecommons.org/licenses/by-nd/2.0/legalcode

"The most important thing in communication is hearing what isn't being said."
S.L. Adler

Great relationships require great communication. Great communication requires that I..

Listen to what is said. Listen for what isn't said. Seek the essence. Validate. Fully understand the other. Only then choose a response.

Convey compassion, warmth, and concern by attending to volume, tone, and body language. Summarize mine and the others viewpoints. Come from a place of creating possibilities and positive outcomes. Speak my "truth" and know it may be different from someone else's truth (and that is okay) because great relationships are based on mutual understanding not on mutual agreement.

How can you improve your understanding?

The Only Direct Way

Photo by Tambako The Jaguar
Mother Gorilla with Baby
https://creativecommons.org/licenses/by-nd/2.0/legalcode

"Just do it!" "Give me!" "Would you!" "Could you!"

What do these statements have in common? They are not direct ways to get your needs met. Remember fulfilling your needs is your primary responsibility, not someone else's.

To get your need met.
Identify it.
If possible meet it for yourself.
Manage your environment.
Take care of you.

If not, put your need into descriptive language…
    "I'm cold"
Then ask directly for what you need.
    "Will you hand me my coat?"
Then acknowledge and appreciate yourself or the person that addressed your needs.

"WILL YOU…?" the only two words in the English language for DIRECTLY asking for what you want.

How will you be direct today?

Boundaries are Invisible Things

Photo by Tambako The Jaguar
Playing Cub II
https://creativecommons.org/licenses/by-nd/2.0/legalcode

Boundaries are funny things. Often invisible. They have to be set. Cannot always be seen. Vary from person to person.

Boundaries getting crossed?

Try this ...

Set the boundary before it gets crossed. Not quick enough? Inform them they have crossed thee... line. Be direct. "Will you...?" Educate. "When you...then I..." Cite the consequences... "If you...then ..."

Learn to say ..."No." Don't explain, or justify your boundaries. It's your life and your limits!

Effective boundaries, start with clarity.

Experience a lack of response to your limit setting? Restate, no response, then leave this is a relationship you don't want.

Where do you need to let go of a relationship?

The Wind Beneath Who's Wings? Create Synergy

Photo by Andrew Morffew
Two Fledged One More to Go
https://creativecommons.org/licenses/by-nd/2.0/legalcode

Really, you want a relationship? Why?

Misery... it will make you happy.

Illness... it will cure you.

Broken... it will fix you.

Suppose to ... it will make you fit in.

Boredom... it will create excitement for you.

Loneliness... it will be company.

Fulfillment... it will fill you up.

Lack purpose... it will give you a reason to be.

Distraction... relief from living your life.

Newsflash! Relationships will not help any of the above. In fact given time they will only magnify these issues for you!

People mistake having a relationship for having a better life. Relationships are a dime a dozen. Just go on line, join a dating service, and you can meet all kinds of people trying to use relationships to fix their lives.

A great relationship takes a great deal more than finding a relationship. To have a better life you have to...

Heal. Grow. Focus. Find. Fulfill your life purpose. Live your life on purpose. Live the happy, healthy relationship with yourself that you want to have with others, when you do, healthy relationships will show up for you. These relationships will add to the *wind beneath your wings*, and you will add to the *wind beneath their wings*. This synergy will allow you both to fly higher, and achieve more, than either of you ever dreamed of doing. What are you really searching for...?

Reflections

From Your Relationships

The Kindness of Telling Your Truth

Photo by Tambako The Jaguar
Lailek Terrorizing Liska Again!
https://creativecommons.org/licenses/by-nd/2.0/legalcode

Have you ever found yourself telling people what you think they want to hear because you want to be *nice*? The excuse you tell yourself is that you don't want to hurt their feelings, when you really mean is you do not want to feel uncomfortable speaking the truth.

Being nice is at best apathetic and at worst cowardly! What *"no, I am really a very nice person!"* Think about it! First, being nice when it isn't your truth is lying. Lies indicate you do not value the relationships. Lies deteriorate intimacy and destroy personal connections. You are better than that and so are they. If they are not, then why do you have them in your life?

Second, you are only responsible for managing your own feelings around telling your truth, you are not responsible for anyone else's feelings.

You do not have the power to control someone else's feelings. Any more than they have the power to control yours.

Third, do you fear that you won't be loved or liked? Have people punished you historically for telling your truth? If you have to change your truth to be loved or liked than you have compromised yourself, and who then are they really loving? You or the you they want you to be?

Respect your own truth, and respect others enough to tell then your truth in a kind way. You will honor yourself and others when you are brave enough to tell them your truth. The truth told with love and caring is the greatest gift that we can offer others.

What kind truths do you need to tell?

Reflections

From Your Relationships

Role Awareness Improves Relationships

Photo by Eric Kilby
Grivet Monkey Family Grooming
https://creativecommons.org/licenses/by-sa/2.0/legalcode

Relationships can be difficult at the best of times. An important thing to remember is your role in the relationship. Is the relationship a peer to peer relationship? Parent to child? Is it a boss to employee relationship? Is it a friend to friend relationship? Is it potential love relationship? Is it a love or monogamous partner relationship?

The role you decide to play in any particular relationship can shift easily. Consider..

The words that are spoken. How words are spoken. Body language. Behaviors. Actions. Inaction. What is said. What isn't said. Who leads. Who follows.

Relationships are constantly negotiated, and roles re-defined.

The role of each person when clear, and well articulated is easy to negotiate. Often the reason things get difficult in relationships is because the contract is not clear between individuals. Clear roles, and articulation of changes in this role are helpful, especially in new relationships. Asking permission to shift roles is a wonderful way to negotiate a shift.

For example, a husband to wife, "May I put on my business hat on here?" If she says, "No." Respect the, "no." Stay in the supportive husband role. If she says, "yes," then by all means put on your business hat.

Remember when you stop that role let your partner know that you have taken off that hat. It feels a bit awkward at first but with practice it makes communication much clearer and strengthens your relationship. Where do your roles need to be clearer?

Reflections

From Your Relationship

You can be Right or You can be Loved!
(J. Gottman) Your Choice!

Photo by Tambako The Jaguar
Lion Snuggle
https://creativecommons.org/licenses/by-nd/2.0/legalcode

Personally, I think being "right" is overrated. I mean what is "right' anyway? "Right" is a concept. "Right" is where your perception lies. Depending on where you stand that perspective looks different. Perspective is forged from life experience. Life experience is the tapestry of all that you encountered, conquered, learned, and loved in your life. The lessons you have chosen to take with you. Therefore, perspective is always changing, your understanding of what is "right" is evolving over time.

If your ego strength is in tact you can both validate the other person's perspective while acknowledging your own. For example, "I can see from your experience why you think that is true," or "I can agree to disagree with you." The reality is not everyone has to agree with you for you to be okay. In fact, the more okay you can be without other people having to agree with you the easier life will get. So, the next time you feel the need to be "right" ask yourself "Why do I have to be right?" Take 20 minutes to free write about it and see what insights emerge for you. What did you find out about yourself?

Do Your Intense Emotions Interfere with Effective Communication?

Photo by Tambako The Jaguar
Pelican Shaking the Water IX
https://creativecommons.org/licenses/by-nd/2.0/legalcode

During a difficult conversation with someone have you ever become overwhelmed with emotions (flooding), or withdraw, and can no longer speak (stonewalling)? This is a familiar pattern for many couples during heated conversations regarding sensitive subjects. These intense emotional states can be referred to as stonewalling or flooding.

Stonewalling occurs when you shutdown, withdraw, and no longer can speak. It is frequently used to avoid becoming overwhelmed or flooded with emotions outwardly; however, inwardly you may be feeling like you are going to lose control. You may think or feel you are trying to be "neutral" but stonewalling conveys disapproval, disconnection, and sometimes contempt to others.

Flooding is most noticeable when there is an outward intense display of emotions. If you are experiencing being flooded you may feel like you drowning in your emotions. Your tears or anger are overwhelming and you are unable to outwardly or inwardly regulate your emotions.

Unfortunately stonewalling and flooding behaviors result in ineffective communication with others. When either stonewalling or flooding occurs you are unable to track what is going on with the other person. So although they serve as self protection from intense psychological arousal they also prevent you from being able to take in the information that might be helpful in resolving issues in the relationship.

Intense physiological arousal prevents you from hearing and communicating clearly with those you care about. In fact when your diffuse physiological arousal reaches high enough states you cannot take in data so you are unable to accurately hear what the other person is saying.

It would be nice if you could simply stop experiencing intense feelings during difficult conversations because you now realize it is ineffective for resolving conflict. Unfortunately this is not the case for most of us. So when you are experiencing a great deal of emotions during a difficult conversation you might want to tell the other person that you need a time-out from the conversation because what is being said is important to you but you are unable to hear in this moment.

Let the other person know that you will come back and talk about the issue later. Giving them a time frame is helpful, for example, 20 minutes, tomorrow morning, after dinner then be sure to follow up. Now it is time to reground, self-soothe, and re-center yourself. There are numerous ways that may work for you. Here are a few ideas you might try.

- Take a walk.
- Take a hot shower or warm bath.
- Meditate.
- Focus on slowing your breathing down.
- Work on a hobby.
- Use a progressive relaxation exercise.
- Close your eyes and envision being in your favorite vacation spot.
- Put on some uplifting music.
- Dance.
- Make a gratitude list. Remember all the little things.

Experiment and figure out what works for you. Remember the idea is to decrease the intensity of your internal physiological arousal until you are in a place where you can resume the conversation with the other person, and hopefully come to a place of understanding and possibly resolution about a difficult issue.

Make a list of what works for you? What else might work?

Photo by Tambako The Jaguar
Resting Wet Pelican
https://creativecommons.org/licenses/by-nd/2.0/legalcode

Surround Yourself with Those that Love You not Need You

Photo by Liam Quinn
King Penguins at Salisbury Plain
https://creativecommons.org/licenses/by-sa/2.0/legalcode

Any time we make a change in our lives, others in our human herd will either encourage us, or discourage us in making progress in our personal growth and life goals. If they have a specific limiting belief about us they will continue to try to pull us back into that specific false belief [I am not ...(you fill in the blank)] about ourselves. if You Have People in your life like this GET RID of THEM... or at the very least MINIMIZE your TIME with THEM.

Instead surround yourself with people that support your growth and change, people that challenge you to move out of your comfort zone and reach your potential. When you enter into any relationship it should be to give AND you will notice that if you are in healthy relationships you will also receive because they are also in it to give not to receive. Wow! What an awesome concept...Both people giving not out of need or necessity but because they desire to serve each other. Now that is where real love and growth begin.

Who will you spend more time with today?

Additional Titles and Information

Visit

www.amaraquest.com

www.ingramcontent.com/pod-product-compliance
Lightning Source LLC
Chambersburg PA
CBHW041608220426
43667CB00001B/7